MW01490266

Copyright © 2025 by Dorothy Smith

All rights reserved.

Book cover by Deanna Bussard

Book cover inspiration: https://www.istockphoto.com/vector/boy-hold-shining-little-planet-earth-in-his-hand-friendly-kid-hug-and-take-care-gm1357529149-431406328

Illustrations by Joanna King

ISBN: 9798316180400

Introduction

He was there that Sunday. He hadn't ever come before nor did he ever come again. Maybe someone had invited him. Maybe he was just curious. I never thought to ask him, "Why?" If I had, no doubt in my mind he would have said, "God told me."

Our song service was over and the Pastor asked if there were any testimonies. Several spoke up and shared what God had done to help, to remedy, to provide, to bless with His joy. Pastor then scanned the congregation and asked if anyone else had praise. From the back of the church came a deep accented voice, "I want to tell you my story of how God saved my life." Pastor asked him to come to the front.

As he came down the center aisle, I recognized him but didn't know anything about him. He began his story with, "I am a heart transplant recipient and alive today because of a miracle God did for me over sixty years ago. I was born on the Greek island of Chios and I lived through the German occupation during World War 2".

Even after many, many years of speaking English, he wasn't easy to understand, but his story was so compelling. When finally, he had finished, the Pastor thanked him. Maybe we applauded, I don't remember. Pastor called the worship team back to the platform – no sermon that day – for a last hymn and closing prayer.

A few people came to him and thanked him for coming and invited him to return. Others commented on his story. I was in that line waiting for my turn. I told him his story needed to be published, and that he should get someone to write it for him.

He looked straight into my eyes and said, "Will you write it for me?"

Only in my daydreams am I a writer. Nevertheless, pure ego took over and I said," Yes, I will." So began over two years of his coming to my kitchen table every couple of weeks and staying about an hour and a half. He told me many things, not in any order. Sometimes about life in his village, sometimes about his adult life in this country, some of which didn't fit in my box of understanding. I would then ask questions as to how, or why. Most times his answer was, "Because that's just the way it was." Some things I have since researched and found he was right – that's the way it was.

It has taken me a very long time to put his words to paper, to do justice to his story, and to take the edge off of the spilled blood, starvation, and death he witnessed as a child. Soon there will be no more people alive who have lived through World War 2 and can testify to the truth of what happened.
Therefore, <u>Because God Loves Me: Costa's World</u> is historical fiction written to inform and entertain.

Because God Loves Me...

COSTA'S WORLD

Acknowledgements

To my daughter, Lynne, who encouraged the publishing of this work.

To my lifelong friends, Marcia and Lowell, who read it, loved it, and asked what happened next?

To my friend, Darese, who "put the writing under a microscope" to locate remaining mechanical errors.

To Deanna and Joanna whose artistic talents have given uniqueness to the project.

And to my Lord Jesus Christ who is before all things, and in Him all things hold together. Colossians 1:17

Table of Contents

Additional Information

As Far Back as I Can Remember

I followed him out the door into the dark night not knowing what he was going to do with the bundle. He held it straight out in front of him, perpendicular to his body, his right hand cupped up under the front and his left under the end close to his chest. He lifted my less than an hour old baby brother to the crescent moon and said, "This is my son. I will call him Petros, Peter."

Earlier in the evening the midwife had arrived and my parents' bedroom door had been closed to Father and me. Now the door was open and the midwife was in and out as she tended to Mother's needs. My father, Sotorious, Stephen, Moushouri, laid Peter on the bed beside his wife, Evangelica. "Now we have two fine sons," he declared. I knelt by the bedside with my chin on the mattress and stared into the face of this tiny being – amazed. I felt my mother's eyes on me and looked up into her smiling face. She whispered the answer to my unasked question:

"Costa, this is God's gift to us."

This special gift had to have come from a special Person and His name was God. Even though I had no words to express it - my third birthday was nine days away - I think right then I began to understand who God is. I have no memories of anything that happened before that March 16, 1940, awe-inspiring night. My memory reaches back only as far as then. However, the wonder of that night didn't last long. Shortly after Peter's birth, my father left for the Merchant Marines. Five of his brothers had done the same and were fighting the Germans in Africa. After his departure, my father never lived with us again. I don't know if he wrote to my mother or his parents. I think he returned to our island village, Vrontados, on Chios, once or twice, but he was a stranger to Peter and me and did nothing to change that.

Grandfather, my father's father, became the male role model in my life. Because the six families of his six sons in the Merchant Marines had been left behind, Grandfather had the job of looking after them and helping his two daughters. Mother, Peter and I lived the closest to Grandfather's house, and Mother did house cleaning for him and my grandmother. I didn't know her well because she was often ill. Later I understood she was a diabetic.

From the time I was out of diapers, could walk the land and not get lost, and had more language, I went with Grandfather. He used every task to teach me something. My first lesson in mending fences started with a question, "Costa, there is a break in the fence. How do you think we can fix it?"

"Put the broken ends together?"

"How can that be done?"

"Grandfather, I don't know what will make the wires stick together."

At that, he laughed and pulled pliers from his back pocket and a small roll of wire from his jacket pocket. Whether it was doing farm chores, visiting his brothers, or going into the village, I was at his side.

I felt so proud the day Grandfather told me, "I have a job that only a very dependable person can do. Costa, can you be that person?"

"Yes, Grandfather, I can." And so he gave me the big responsibility – only me, Constantine Sotorious Moushouri.

New Things

The strings hung around my neck with right shoe shoestrings tied to left shoe shoestrings. My shoes, stuffed with socks, banged against my chest as I ran barefoot through the fields. Mother told me not to get into mud or wade in water with my new –new to me- shoes. My cousin had outgrown them before the shoes wore out. Mother said I would probably do the same; then the shoes could be given to Peter. At that moment I wasn't concerned with shoes. I had a job to do that helped Grandfather and saved him time. I was surrounded by his thirty acres of tillable ground. Grandfather grew everything or so I thought then: grains for people and animals, figs, pomegranates, quinces, persimmons, grapes, and nuts in addition to raising cows, chickens, and a few horses.

Our Island was beautiful but very dry in the late summer. Therefore, a responsible person was needed to do a necessary job. Grandfather said I was just that person. I ran beside the stream for a short distance and found the irrigation shut-off valve then opened it. I stepped both feet into the cool water as it flowed into the ditches. Grandfather would come later in the morning and close the valve.

That task completed; my thoughts turned to my next destination - school. It wasn't far and I ran until I was across the road from it. I stopped at a grassy spot to brush the dirt from my feet and put on the required socks and shoes. I walked up the school steps with purpose and through the door for the first time ever. Mother had begun to teach me to read, but now I would learn so much more.

A smiling teacher greeted me and led me to my classroom. Excitement bubbled within as I sat down. There was so much to see in this room. My joy was halted by a large framed picture of a sad faced man holding a sharp knife above the chest of a boy lying on a rock wall. The boy's expression questioned the man. I couldn't look away. The teacher stood beside me and said my name. I didn't respond. Her gaze followed mine to the wall and the picture.

"Costa, do you know the story of this picture?"

"No."

"It is from the book of Genesis in the Bible. Sometime we will read it together, but for now I will tell you a little bit of it. God asked the man, Abraham, to do a very hard thing. The boy, Isaac, his son, trusted his father.

Look in the background of the picture, Costa. Do you see a goat with its horns tangled in briers? God told Abraham to stop what he was doing and look behind him. Isaac got up from the stone table and helped his father capture the goat. God provided the goat which was exactly what Abraham needed to do what God had asked him to do. Costa, when you look at this picture or think about it, remember the message: God will provide."

Content with that explanation, I settled into the work of kindergarten. It was the goat that drew my attention each time I looked at the picture. I did not yet know the details of the story, but knew enough to know the goat's life was taken not Isaac's because God provides.

Not Fishing

I could see him standing at the gate to his house talking to someone. I knew he wouldn't forget we were going fishing. As I came closer, I heard Grandfather yelling; using words he didn't often use. Now I recognized Grandfather's brother who seldom visited. After listening, my great uncle Michael threw up his hands and stalked away. I stood beside Grandfather, tipped my head back, looked into his troubled face, and asked, "Are you taking me fishing?"

"Maybe, but first I need to go into the village. You can come, if you like, or you can wait until I get back."

"I want to go. Grandfather, are you angry with your brother? He looked sad when he walked away."

"I am angry, Costa, but not with any of my family. Come. Try to keep up with me."

Several times Grandfather had to stop and wait for me to catch up. He didn't seem to mind, but something was bothering his mind. He directed our way to the village square where there was a large group of people, mostly men. Again, I heard loud, angry voices and words not often shouted. Grandfather moved his way through the crowd to an over-sized piece of paper nailed to a tree. Just then a policeman came beside Grandfather, but he turned toward the assembled people and said, "Friends, there is no need to be upset. The government wants you to store your guns at the police station. That's what this paper says. Just bring your guns here and they will be safe."

Someone in the crowd yelled, "We are hunters. We need our guns."

I had been hunting with Grandfather when he was looking for rabbits. Sometimes we were after partridge.

"That's no problem." responded the officer, "When you need them, come get them." Then his voice became less friendly, "I am following orders from my superiors, and you must obey. See to it that you meet the deadline and there will be no regrets." He turned his back and strode away as if that settled that.

Grandfather's large hand squeezed my shoulder, "No fishing today, Costa," he spoke solemnly, "but I do need your help. Let's go home."

I had no idea what was happening. The men of the village were angry and guns were the reason. I knew it was best to not ask questions now. I would wait for Grandfather's directions. The first one came before we got to his gate, "Costa, go to the shed at the edge of the pasture and get the papers and the bucket of rags that are just inside the door. Take them to the kitchen."

By the time I had done that, Grandfather and his brother Michael were in the kitchen. Another of Grandfather's brothers, George, entered from the front of the house as I came in the back.   Each man had a gun in each hand, and the tabletop was covered with rifles. For a few seconds no one said anything. Then Uncle George said, "Well, which ones do we give to the police station?"

"The firing pin is bent in this one. They can have it. And this one is only for close range. There, two should make me the model citizen," sneered Uncle Michael.

"Demetri, what about you," questioned Uncle George pointing at the table, "More than half of these are yours."

Grandfather scanned the array of weapons, laughed sarcastically, and picked up an especially old looking one. Holding it vertically at arm's length, he threatened, "If any of them try to use this against us, it is so deteriorated with rust that it is likely to explode in his face."

Uncle George explained which gun he would hand in, but I was focused on what Grandfather had said, "If any of them should try to use this against us…" Who was "them", and who was "us"? In another second I realized Grandfather's brothers were going out the back door and there were fewer guns on the table.

"Now the work begins, Costa. We must grease these guns with pig fat and wrap them in paper. Next we will put them in these burlap bags, and the bags will go in these crates George brought." explained Grandfather.

"I don't understand. Don't you and your brothers need them?"

"Costa, we were told today that every gun must be turned into police headquarters. It is a new law. We were also told we can get them when we need them. That may be true, but we are preparing if it is not true." While he talked, he silently showed me how to wrap each gun – his and his brothers. The guns were divided between the two crates, and grandfather nailed on the lids.

"Is our work done, Grandfather? Did you forget lunch?"

"No, to both questions." laughed Grandfather, "We have to wait until after dark to do the last thing. And as for lunch, there is bread and cheese in the cupboard."

"Will you ask Mother if I can help you? She will tell me it will be past my bedtime. And what are we going to do, and why do we have to wait for dark?"

"Oh, Costa! I will talk to your mother. Eat your lunch and no more questions!"

That afternoon I helped my mother by keeping an eye on Peter. He surely could run fast for a toddler. After supper all thoughts of helping Grandfather were out of my mind. As my mother helped me into bed, all I wanted was sleep.

Church and Birthday

When I was fully awake, I remembered it was Sunday and we would be going to church. I had trouble sitting quietly through the service, but Mother's little pinches applied to the back of my arm were a frequent reminder of proper behavior. My cousins would be there too – my aunts had also perfected "the pinch" to settle disruptions before they started. After service we had about a half an hour to play together while the mothers talked; then each child's name was called with the order, "Time to go home."

There was more to smile about. This was March and this week was Peter's birthday and mine was nine days later. Since they were so close, both birthdays were celebrated at the same time. Peter was going to be one year old and I, turning four, looked forward to getting a gift from Grandfather. "Grandfather! What had he done with the crates?" I ran downstairs, out the back door, and straight to Grandfather's house.

He saw me coming and opened the door. Immediately I saw there were no crates. "Grandfather, what was the last thing? Where are the crates?"

"The last thing was burying them in the fields after dark hoping no one saw me. But you must not tell anyone what we did with the guns, promise me, Costa?"

"I do promise, but I wanted to help you. Will you show me where you put them?"

"No. If you don't know, you can't tell. Now forget all about guns, ok?"
"Yes, Grandfather."

"Well then, go home and do your chores," ordered Grandfather.

After gathering a few eggs, carrying three my size buckets of water, and eating a quick breakfast, we were off to church in the village. Mother pushed Peter in his stroller and I walked or skipped beside her. Saint Isidoros Orthodox Church was about in the center of Vrontados. Having to sit still gave me a lot of time to really look at all the trappings that filled the walls and ceiling of the sanctuary. My imagination roamed when I stared at the picture of my saint, Isidoros. He was mounted on a sturdy horse that appeared to have suddenly been pulled to a stop. Saint Isidoros held the reins in his right hand and a long spear – the tip of it all but touched the ground – was managed by his left arm and hand. I supposed he was declaring to the enemy, "I will not allow you to harm my people." Other times, I sent Saint Isidoros into the battle to destroy the foe. And so, time passed until the end of the service.

Before joining my cousins, I wanted to ask Grandfather if he would take me fishing. He was already talking with a group of men including his brothers. I ran to the group but stopped short of them when I heard the word, "Resistance." I had asked what that word meant and Grandfather explained, "It is Greek people doing everything they can to keep the Italians from taking over our country. Costa, don't worry your mind about this. Leave it to the grown-ups." That was my answer and caution to not ask again. Turning away, I ran to play before Mother called, "Time to go home."

The next Saturday Grandfather took me fishing. It was supper time until we got home, I ran in the kitchen to show Mother the fish I had caught and was surprised to see Grandmother there. She smiled and said, "Happy Birthday, Costa."

Grandfather and Grandmother stayed for supper and Mother served cake for dessert. Dessert was nearly unheard of in our house. Then Grandfather handed me an odd shaped brown paper wrapped package. It was a slingshot.

Bad News

Grandfather and the men of the village were sure the Greek army, with the help of the resistance, was pushing the Italians out of Greece. From Grandfather I had learned there was a big war happening, but it was far away and not affecting us.

In the afternoon on an April Sunday, when Grandfather was sitting on the back porch, I was playing with cousins who had come with us from church. Great Uncle George suddenly appeared. Before Grandfather could ask why he had come, George blurted out, "The Germans have crossed the Albanian border to help the Italians! Our army has already retreated from the position they had held."

"Maybe they just need to regroup and then counter attack," responded Grandfather.

"Perhaps you are right. I pray you are right, Demetri. We must listen to the radio tonight."

Then he was gone.

During the day there was school for me, and Grandfather had the spring crops to plant. At night he listened to the radio report as did my mother and anyone who had a radio. The BBC broadcast from London, England was after my bedtime, but I heard the adults talk and understood that the Greek army was no match for the Germans.

Three weeks after Uncle George told us about the Germans helping the Italians, we were in church singing, when our priest stopped us. A man I recognized as one of Grandfather's friends had just run to the front of the church and whispered to the priest who announced. "It is bad news," he told us, "The Germans have entered our capital, Athens, with no resistance. The Nazi flag is now flying from the Acropolis."

Our lives continued as usual, but everyone was carrying a heavy burden of "what is next."

Early May, 1941: "Demetri! Demetri! Demetri, come now!" shouted three different voices over the sound of running feet.

Grandfather was out of the house and through the gate before I could think, "Run too." He paused long enough for me to catch up and we both saw the backs of the men walking fast – running toward the village. The police station was the destination. By the time we got there, the men were a roaring mob. Some yelled, "We were told we could have them when we wanted them!"

Others screamed, "What do you mean there are no guns here. We gave them to the police and we want them!" Every man, some with fists beating the air, was bursting with verbal anger. The man standing in front of the police station was not a policeman. There were no policemen anywhere. When it seemed the men of the village were on the verge of tearing down the police station, the mayor appeared.

"Men of Vrontados!" his booming voice got their attention. "It is obvious you have heard that the German ships are headed to our harbor. We, here, had no say in taking your guns nor did we have any control when your guns were collected and taken from here. Soon the Germans will be the policemen. I give you this advice; Men between the ages of sixteen and fifty should go to the mountains. The others stay." In silence, the men walked away. They respected the mayor, and they knew; they just knew.

The First Taste

Whereas Athens was deserted - the government fled, the people fled, or people stayed behind locked doors, and the streets were empty when the Nazis rolled triumphantly into the capital - the adults in my world decided to go about day-to-day life normally to show the Germans we were not intimidated. The German ships docked in our harbor and the army and the tanks were set ashore first. While the men took positions on the street corners, the tanks were placed in the roads leading into Vrontados.

In the village a few women shopped at the open market. Men sat in the barber shop, some on the street benches, and others at Moushouri Coffee Shop. Sometimes people stopped to talk to one another briefly and then moved on. Other than me, there were maybe half a dozen children playing nearby. I stayed close to Grandfather. Two of his brothers and other men of the village meandered into the town square. Within an hour Vrontados was under German occupation. The men became silent when the top commanders of the invading force motored up to the flagpole in the square.

I remember the details of that day. The German officer in charge gave the order to take down the Greek flag. A soldier responded and then threw the flag to the ground and stomped on it. I saw it happen, but it was all so fast maybe I didn't see it. Maybe I only know because the adults have told the story. As the German soldier's foot was raised to stomp again, Uncle George spit in the soldier's face. While the spit was still landing, the German officer pulled out his pistol and shot Uncle George in the head. Grandfather pushed the back of my head into the side of his thigh and I heard the thump as Uncle George's body hit the ground.

Grandfather whirled my body around away from the direction of the sound and pushed me to move forward. In a fraction of a second, in the turn I made, I saw what my mind did not understand. "Get the body out of here!" must have been the next order given. Only many years later was I able to put the sights and sounds of that happening together and know. Grandfather kept me moving until we turned on the road that led home. Then he picked me up and carried me home. No words.

I don't know how my family dealt with the Germans to arrange it, but there was a funeral for Uncle George. We mourned his loss. This was the first bitter taste of more to come.

The First Taste

They Are Everywhere – Don't Forget It!

Second to having removed the Greek flag, the Germans posted the list of their demands on trees, on buildings, on roughly made signs that led to small outlying neighborhoods of Vrontados. No one could use the excuse of not knowing. I heard the lists discussed by the adults, but only a few affected me; the curfew was unfair. Summer evenings were not even dark by eight o'clock! Radios and motorized vehicles had to be taken to the German controlled police station. Anyone caught trying to hide either was arrested. After a few days of collecting, the Germans began a house-to-house search.

It was a warmer than usual day in May, and Grandfather had me planting flowers for Grandmother. "Costa, that's not a hole. It's a dip. Dig deeper."

"How deep is deeper, Grandfather?"

"Turn the flower pot upside down, hold the stem, and slowly pull out the flower. See the root. All of that and a little more go underground."

"So when I plant flowers, I measure the root first to know how deep to dig?"

"Maybe at first, but after some practice you will be an expert without measuring. You have five to plant. Costa, get digging," ended Grandfather and he went into the house.

The door hadn't completely closed when the sound of motors filled the air. Grandfather came back as four soldiers and their commander also came into the yard.

Motioning to the four soldiers, the commander ordered, "Search the house." Grandfather took a step toward the door, but the German yelled, "Stop!" and aimed his pistol at Grandfather's heart, and said, "You did not bring your radio to us." I saw the hammer move back slightly.

Just then the soldiers returned with Grandfather's radio. "Where did he have it hidden?" smirked the German in poor Greek.

"It wasn't hidden. It was sitting on a table in the living room," responded a soldier.

"I was planning to bring it to you this afternoon," explained Grandfather, "but you came before I could do that."

The gun was holstered, the command to go was given, and Grandfather was alive. He took my hand, stood me to my feet, and quietly said, "Time for lunch."

Neither of us had spoken, but the silence was broken by Aunt Mary, Uncle George's widow, calling "Demetri, I need you," as she opened the door. Grandfather beckoned her to sit down. She was pale and shaking. Her black mourning dress gave her a ghostly look. "The Germans, the Germans...," she began.

The Germans had been to her house before coming to our area. Aunt Mary explained she had not opened the door when they pounded and demanded entry, but they entered uninvited, grabbed her right arm, pulled it behind her back, and demanded to know why she hadn't responded to the door. Thinking she was going to be killed, Aunt stuttered out, "I, I was – at the toilet." She was slammed against the wall and fell to the floor, but she was alive. The soldiers pulled out drawers, with the sweep of one black gloved hand emptied cupboard shelves, and threw the contents of closets on the floor, but found no radio. Perhaps angry because they had found nothing, they smashed a few things on their way out. Aunt Mary didn't move from the floor for more than a half an hour to make sure the Germans had truly gone.

"Mary, you are alive. That's more than..." Grandfather caught himself and didn't finish the sentence.

"Yes, Demetri. But that's not why I came. When George heard the Germans would soon be in Vrontados, he hid the radio saying, 'First the guns then the radios so we only know what they tell us.' I want you to get the radio and you can tell us the truth. I fear the soldiers may come back and find it."

Grandfather allowed me to go with him that evening. When it was fully dark, we went behind Aunt Mary's house where Uncle George had a large rock pile for adding to the stone wall he was building. Grandfather walked around it once keeping his lantern close to the ground; then he did that again. That time he stooped down and moved several extra-large rocks. "Costa, bring the sack." I knelt beside him and opened the sack while he lifted the radio from its entombment and slid it in. He extinguished the lantern flame, replaced the rocks, and took me home. I fell asleep wondering where Grandfather would hide the radio.

Broken to Pieces

I voiced my opinion that the curfew was unfair and my mother immediately silenced me with the explanation that I should practice keeping my mouth closed so I would not be caught complaining about the Germans. That led to my asking her questions about their rules and so I was given answers about curfew, banning radios and even why the Germans were collecting motorized vehicles and sinking them in the ocean. I understood her words, but the ideology behind them was lost on me.

Mother said I needed a break from Grandfather so for the next few days I went to school, did my chores, and played with Peter. When I could again spend time with him, the first question I asked was, "Where did you hide the radio and why didn't you hide your radio so the Germans won't take it?"

"Second question first," began Grandfather, "Your Grandmother asked me to plant those few flowers just as I was about to hide the radio. That's why it was still sitting on the table. I left it to get you to do the planting job. I didn't expect the Germans to show up so soon, but maybe that was a blessing because now they are not as likely to come again and search. Costa, you know the answer to where I hid Uncle George's radio. If you don't…"

"…know, you can't tell," I finished his sentence.

"Right, however I will show you something I have hidden." He turned, motioned me to follow, and walked toward the barn.

Once inside, Grandfather closed the door and started pitchforking hay off of a pile taller than I was to another spot on the floor. My eyes had adjusted to the dim light and I saw a piece of canvas appearing from under the hay and quickly realized it was covering some large thing. I was shocked into a speechless frozen state when Grandfather lifted a motorbike to its standing position.

I moved forward to touch it while questions tumbled from my mouth tripping over each other in unintelligible babble. Grandfather laughed and then asked, "Do you think this is a good hiding place or do you think when the Germans come searching for whatever they can find, they will find this?" I gave no answer so Grandfather did, "They will find it and my family will be in danger. So, you and I will take it apart and hide the pieces."

I really was too stunned to ask any questions. As a matter of fact it was near the end of the war that I finally asked, "Where did that motorcycle come from?" It was a BMW 1927 model R37 that a young Swiss man brought with him when he bought a small house in the area. He had wrecked once or twice but that didn't stop him from speeding around the island. It was the stock market crash (Grandfather had to stop and explain that to me) that forced him to return to Switzerland. He sold his house and looked for someone to buy his bike. Among the men who wanted it, only Grandfather had the bargaining power – the motor cut out too often and rust had a strong influence on its appearance - and the money to buy it. Grandfather had kept it hidden in the barn and worked on it when he could.

Rather than allow the Germans the pleasure of sinking the bike in the ocean, we took the wheels off first, then the motor was taken off the frame. "Grandfather, why don't we build a box from those boards you have thrown in that corner - to hide the frame?"

"If the Germans walked in here and saw a big wooden box, the first thing they would do would be smash it open."

"What if we laid the frame on the floor and piled the boards on top of it?"

"If the boards formed a frame around the bike like a house foundation, and then other boards were laid across the top that would cover it. Costa, you are thinking hard about this I know, but anything that looks out of the ordinary will draw the soldiers' attention."

The barn floor was resting on a stone foundation that gave a three-foot clearance between the floor and the earth below. Grandfather removed several floor boards and laid the bike on the dirt. The floorboards fit tightly together without nails.

I helped Grandfather take grain from the bin so he could put one wheel in the bottom of the bin and then I covered the wheel with grain. The other wheel was hung on the wall in plain sight. Grandfather pounded nails in the wall above the wheel and hung ropes, worn out leather straps, and old rusty chains on the nails. The wheel disappeared under the old junk.

Grandfather wrapped the motor in rags and put it into a sack. I held the sack open while he filled it with ears of field corn. To my surprise, Grandfather left the sack sitting on the floor by the door. Grandfather thanked me and said, "This is one vehicle they will wish they had sunk."

You Have No Rights

Mother knew everything. Maybe Grandfather told her. Maybe I told her. Somehow, she knew things. Mother, Peter and I were finishing supper when I asked, "Mother, where do you think Grandfather hid the radio?"

"Where do you think he hid it? Think about it, Costa. Would he hide it in the barn?"

"No. Someone might see him getting it or taking it back and tell the Germans."

"So if it is not outside, he must have…"

"Put it in the house where he can get it easily and put it back in hiding quickly."

"Next time you are there, look around for anything that looks different. Your Grandfather is very clever and so are you."

"Did you ever see Grandfather riding a motorbike, Mother?"

"That's a strange question, Costa, but the answer is yes, a long time ago. The bike was dented and had some rust. It would run for a few miles then the motor would sputter to a stop. I supposed Grandfather put it on the junk pile. How did you know to ask about something that happened years before you were born?"

"Oh." No excuse I made satisfied her. So, the truth, the whole truth, came out. She listened to every word and when I finished my story, she still was silent. I remember thinking I was in big trouble.

"Costa, you know you must not tell anyone – not aunts or cousins or anyone."

"Are you angry with me, Mother? Have I done something wrong? I won't tell."

"No, I am not angry and you are fine."

There was no peaceful settling in with the German occupation. The soldiers came again. This time they were looking for food. They weren't asking us to share. They took everything: grain, vegetables, fruits, cows, goats. If a Greek citizen cooperated with them, maybe he could keep a subsistence amount of food for his family.

When the Germans came to Grandfather's, he tried to stop them from raiding his farm. He told them he was the main supplier for six families. Surely, they could understand. They didn't. "You have no right to take what is mine. You have no right to take what I have worked for. You have no right to take what belongs to my children," yelled Grandfather as he ran at a soldier and knocked a basket of vegetables out of his hand.

The German commander shouted orders for the soldiers to return to the truck that had brought them. To our horror the tank that had accompanied them turned its gun on the fields of corn and grain, and on the vegetable garden. Grandfather's fields were burned.

In Greek this time, the commander calmly said, "There is your answer. You have no rights." It was years until the soil could again grow crops.

Something Missing

The food Grandfather had been providing for his six sons' families was gone. My mother and my aunts each had a small vegetable garden near the house that provided fresh food for the table during the summer, but there was not the needed quantity to preserve for between the growing seasons. Grandfather's land was not the only property burned; several landowners who tried to talk the German out of taking everything lost everything. The message of scorched and chemically poisoned land caused the remaining farmers not to resist in any way. Only those people, collaborators, who were more than willing to spy on their neighbors for the Germans, had food still growing in their gardens and fields.

School was out for the summer and Grandfather found things for me to do. I was helping him remove rocks from a piece of his land he had never cultivated. He hoped to clear it and plant oats. Grandfather threw the rocks into a horse drawn wagon. Most of the rocks were too big for me to lift and pitch so I was the spotter to point out the big rocks.

"Costa, this is more rock under the dirt than on top. If I had my short-handled shovel, I could get it out. I think I left it in the barn. Would you go and get it for me? You might have to look around until you find it because I don't remember exactly where I left it."

Glad to get out of the sun for a while, I answered with, "Yes, I will."

It was cool in the barn and darker than outside. I didn't see the shovel right away, but I did see that the sack of corn with the bike motor in it was gone. Thinking that Grandfather had just moved it, I looked everywhere. I didn't find it, but I did find the shovel. I returned to the field, but I didn't ask about the sack. Grandfather used the shovel as a lever after getting it under the rock. I was his cheering section when the rock popped up from its earthen prison. We called it a day after that.

Later in the afternoon, I was in front of our house trying to keep Peter from eating dirt while Mother trimmed the flower bushes. "Costa," Mother called, "Isn't it fortunate for us that the Germans don't eat flowers." I laughed at the thought of German soldiers picking our flowers and popping them in their mouths, and Peter choked on his fistful of dirt. Mother came running and turned him upside down.

That was when the wagon passed our house. I didn't recognize the driver, but I did recognize the tarp that partially covered the stack of wood in the wagon. I had just seen the tarp in Grandfather's barn tossed beside the hay stack that had covered it. The boards appeared to be neatly stacked in layers – one layer parallel to the sides of the wagon and the next perpendicular. The tarp was tied to the corners formed by the way the wood was stacked.

Mother had taken Peter inside to wash his mouth and I asked, "Mother, I need to check something in Grandfather's barn, ok? I will be right back."

"Quickly, Costa, quickly."

As soon as I walked in, I saw the empty place where the wood had been. There was no wheel hanging on the wall either. I turned a bucket upside down in front of the grain bin, grabbed a broom, stood on the bucket, and opened the bin lid. I stuck the boom handle down in the grain. I did that three times. There was no wheel in that bin. I put everything back where it was and went home.

When I again helped Grandfather pick up rocks, I told him, "Grandfather, when I was in the barn the other day, I saw that the corn sack with the bike motor was gone and so was the wheel on the wall."

"So, they are. Costa, are you asking where I put them?"

"Yes, Grandfather. I want to know."

"They are in a place where they will be useful. That is the only answer I will give you now."

Mother

The Germans used severe intimidation and deadly consequences to keep people in a constant state of paranoia. One of their tactics was to fly low over the island and sometimes use the plane's machine gun to rain down bullets not on any particular target but on whatever or whoever happened to be there. Because of this, the mayor of Vrontados ordered the schools to close for the safety of the children.

During one of those scare tactics, Mother, Peter and I were walking barefoot on the beach. Mother told us how happy she was to have two fine sons just as Peter splashed me and I retaliated with a hand scoop of water that got him in his face and eyes. Peter started to cry. Instead of scolding us, Mother laughed and said, "Peter, when you start it, are you able to take what you give?" I don't think he understood, and Mother made me apologize because, "Costa, you are the oldest and should know better," warned Mother.

Our little drama was interrupted by the sound of an airplane engine. Mother went to her knees, pulled us down to our knees, drew us close, and arched her body over us even as the bullets exploded around us. We shook with fear and Peter cried frantically. I screamed out, "Where is my father! Why did he leave us?"

Mother answered in a strong firm voice, "God is your Father. Do not be afraid. Jesus Christ and Saint Isideros will protect us." The bullets had not stopped, but I felt as if we were in an impenetrable bubble. Then the plane flew away. Mother held Peter and I sat beside her. "The water is so beautiful. Look Peter! It is a beautiful blue." After a few minutes, we walked home.

That evening after Mother had put Peter to bed, I angrily asked, "Why is God letting this happen?" She was silent. I waited. Then she spoke, "God did not start the war, Costa, men did. God allowed it, but He continues to show His compassion through it."

As a child, I didn't understand my mother was a wise woman, but others did. She was also known in our village as a healer and was often called upon to pray over the sick. Evidently God answered her prayers or the people would not have requested her to pray time after time. Through those terrible years, Mother remained strong. She was faithful to find reasons to give God thanks in the midst of the worst of times.

The Beach

Grocery Shopping

It was already dark outside when Grandfather came to our house and asked Mother if I could help him. Whatever he was doing– he didn't explain - he needed someone to hold the light. Mother agreed, but I was expected back in an hour.

I was learning that I needed to wait to ask questions. Grandfather told me that if I waited and listened, most times, I would have an answer before I asked. So, I was practicing that wisdom and it was hard! Grandfather gave me the lantern. The low flame cast light for only a few feet. He carried a half dozen sacks and led the way to his property line between his and his neighbor's land. This neighbor, one of the collaborators - though he denied it, was not a friend of Grandfather. People were polite to this man and his family, but village conversation stopped if he or any of his family came within listening distance.

"We are here, Costa, look." He took the lantern and lifted it above his head. I saw pumpkins, zucchini, cabbage, and a few tomatoes. "It is the grocery store. Let's shop quickly and quietly." He handed me two bags and told me to get the cabbage and zucchini. He set the light on the ground and we shopped. When he filled a bag, he took it across to his property and hid it under a bush. When he saw my sack was too full for me to carry, he took it to the bush. We finished and hurried back to Moushouris' land. I thought our biggest job was ahead – carrying the heavy sack to the house -, but under the bush was Grandfather's wheelbarrow with a rake and another sack in it.

"Costa, we left our footprints. Come, we need to erase them." Where our prints were shallow, Grandfather lightly pulled the rake through and feathered out the dirt. When our footprint was deep, he used the rake to fill in dirt then had me get on my knees and drag the sack over the area as I crawled backwards. "I hope we didn't miss any." Grandfather said as he looked over the store. "It is hard to see with so little light."

I carried a small sack of zucchini and a lantern. Grandfather heaped the others sacks in the wheelbarrow. He pushed his load around the edge of the field, a few feet in where the bushes would branch over the wheelbarrow tracks. Pushing was hard and the going was slow.

When he was beside his house, he was out of breath and sat down on the ground. "Grandfather, are you alright? Can you get up? What can I do to help you?" I was worried. He turned his back to me and faced the stone foundation of his house.

"Hold the lantern here," he pointed to his right side. Then he wriggled a stone loose from the wall in front of him; then another and another and another until the opening was big enough for a filled sack to pass through. Before putting the sacks into the four- foot high space under his house, Grandfather put aside some of each vegetable to take into the house. The sacks were in, the stones replaced, the wheelbarrow back in the barn, and Grandfather said, "Hidden and in a cool dry place. Time to take you home."

Mother asked if I had been helpful, and I looked up at Grandfather. "Oh, very," he told her.

"Just what did you do, Costa?" inquired Mother, looking at Grandfather rather than me.

"I held the light for Grandfather...," I said and Grandfather finished the sentence.

"...while I replaced some missing stones in my house foundation."

"Uh ha. Time to get washed for bed, Costa," and she gave Grandfather a look that said, "I know there is more to this."

Fish Thieves

The Germans didn't destroy the olive groves, but when the olives from the groves were pressed, they took the oil to the Turks and traded it for food for themselves. Grandfather had several olive trees the Germans had bypassed; we were grateful for that. Grandfather did get the rock field cleared and had planted tomatoes and a few vegetables in addition to grain in early spring. It was nearing the middle of September and the produce was divided among seven families according to the number of people in the family. Our food supply came from the land and the sea, but the Germans controlled both.

Grandfather would sometimes allow me to stay at a safe distance from the docks in Vrontados to watch the fishermen returning between four and five o'clock while he was busy in the village. Fishing was a centuries old occupation for the men of Vrontados. Every day their small boats went to sea and when they returned there was fish to feed their families and enough to sell but not in the summer of 1941 and not for the next four summers. When the fishing boats came in, the Germans were waiting. They left nothing. I hoped the fishermen got creative with hiding at least several buckets of fish for their families.

One Saturday afternoon in September I walked to the village with Grandfather. He had a burlap bag slung over his left shoulder and its contents clanged quietly. "Costa, I am meeting friends at Moushouris' Coffee Shop to discuss some business. Our talk will not interest you. Would you like to go to the dock for about an hour?"

"Yes. I like to watch what is happening. Sometimes there are other children to play with. What is making a clanging sound in your sack, and where are you taking it?"

"Some old tools I don't often use and I think my friends might have use for them. I will walk you to the dock first. You must remember to not go any farther than the wall. You have to be careful to not do anything to attract the attention of the soldiers. If it looks like something might even turn into trouble, get out of there quickly."

"Grandfather, you tell me the same thing each time you allow me to watch."

"It is for your safety. Do you understand that?"

"Yes, Sir."

"I will be back for you within an hour."

I could see the tiny dots that were the fishing boats out on the sea. I didn't see any children so I just sat, watching. A German box truck drove onto the dock and men from a cargo ship began loading crates into the back of the truck. The cargo ship must have been German because the workers and the soldiers kept up a lively conversation with intermittent laughter. Still staying on the wall, I moved along it trying to get a look at the crates.

My eyes were on the truck and I didn't see Grandfather come to the wall. My hour wasn't up, but suddenly Grandfather was by my side accompanied by two other men. Grandfather had said, "Friends and business deal." These men looked like they could use a bath, and they were very young. They intently watched the cargo being loaded.

I asked, "Grandfather, do you know what is in those crates? I can see some of the letters stamped on them, but I don't know the word."

"Ammunition is the word, Costa. I guess the Germans think they will need it to keep us under their control."

The truck was loaded and the soldiers dropped the canvas flap down over the rear opening. Then turning to the men, Grandfather said, "Gentlemen, I believe you will be testing our deal to know if it works for you. You know how to contact me."

The men had not spoken one word. They touched their caps and nodded at Grandfather as though they were saying, "Yes, and goodbye," and they left.

By now the tiny dots were the village fishing boats coming into the harbor. "Can we stay long enough to see one boat unload the fish, please, Grandfather?"

"You can stay while I see if there is any coffee left in the village."

I saw that the truck with the ammunition was still on the dock. Another box truck pulled behind it. This time the soldiers from the first truck jumped in the back of the second truck and tossed out metal tubs to the soldiers who had driven the second truck. The first fishing boat with a pile of fish on the deck was secured to the dock. Three soldiers jumped down to its deck and ordered the fishermen to put the fish into the metal tub. I don't even know the direction they came from, but there were soldiers on each boat giving the same order. The fishermen were also ordered to place the tubs in the truck. So much was happening so fast that Grandfather startled me with, "Time to go home, Costa." It was beginning to get dark and "home" sounded good.

It Worked!

A few miles north of Vrontados was the home of another collaborator who had a large barn on his farm. The Germans took over the barn and used it as a warehouse for supplies and ammunition. Guards were posted around the clock every day. I knew this because I heard Grandfather and his brothers and their friends talking about it. Since there was no longer any coffee, the men would drink herbal teas at the coffee shop and talk about local happenings. They were careful not to mention anything that came from the radio broadcast.

I was at Grandfather's house on a cloudy, cold November day drinking hot herbal tea when Grandfather's brother Michael and a friend came in. By the looks on their faces, they had something to tell Grandfather. They didn't seem to mind that I was there too.

"Demetri, the resistance, oh I wish I could have seen it. Nobody knows how they did it, but oh, the blast! The bad part is that now the Germans will do something evil to prove no one can get the best of them."

All this flew from Uncle Michael's mouth at lightning speed, and Grandfather said, "Michael, slow down. You aren't making sense. What ARE you talking about?"

Uncle Michael and his friend sat down and Uncle took a deep breath and said, "Ok, from the beginning. You know the Germans use Matheous's barn as a warehouse. You know when supplies come in to Vrontados the Germans load trucks and drive those winding roads to that barn."

Grandfather shook his head, "Yes," he answered.

Last night in the dark of the moon, at the last twist in the road before the barn came into sight, a motor bike came out of somewhere, roared down the hill and the rider threw an explosive into the back of the truck and kept going to the barn. The guards heard the blast and ran in that direction. The blast noise covered the sound of the motor bike until the bike was almost to the barn. Because the guards had been going away from the barn, they stopped.   In the time it took them to decide which direction to go, the rider threw a second explosive into the barn and escaped into the hills behind it."

Grandfather looked skeptical and asked, "How would you know this wonderful story if you were not there?"

"Demetri, meet my friend, Fotus."

"Michael, you know I know Fotus," Grandfather responded in a slightly irritated tone.

"Yes, but did you know he speaks German well enough to understand most things they say?"

"No, I did not. So, finish the details of this story, please."

Fotus spoke up and continued, "I was in the coffee shop this morning when a group of soldiers came in. They think no one understands German so they speak freely among themselves. What Michael told you is what they said. The two soldiers in the truck died. There was no one in the barn when it blew. However, the German high command is furious. There will be retribution."

Uncle Michael broke in, "Yes, but the motor bike, the motor bike. How could even the resistance have one – did they have it shipped in, did they fly it in, even if someone on the island had one, how did it get past the German's? You know they searched every property looking for motorized vehicles. Even yours, I was here to see you the day they came, but you had taken your wife to the doctor's. Don't you remember what I told you?"

"I do remember. How many others have you told about this?" Grandfather quite seriously inquired. He didn't seem to be in awe of the event as was Michael.

Fotus answered, "We just came from the coffee shop. You and Costa are the only ones we have told. Does it matter?"

"I think you should not tell anyone else and neither will we," said Grandfather looking straight at me. "Consider what the Germans will do if the whole village knows. They will go from person to person until they find the source which is you, Fotus. Have you thought about the value of your ability to understand them and they don't know? I of course don't know how, but if you could contact the resistance and let them know what the Germans talk about, even if you think there is nothing to it, it might help them."

"Demetri, we will keep this to ourselves. What do you think the Germans might do to our people?"

"I don't even want to think about that, but the less the people know the better."

In an unnaturally loud voice, I piped up and said, "You can't tell what you don't know." And I said it with finality.

Strange Visit

November passed and Christmas came. There were homemade presents. Mother took the yarn from a sweater that had been my father's and knitted me a sweater. By this time, I was in need of shoes. Mother had cut the toes of my shoes out so my foot had room to grow; then she wrapped several layers of burlap around the toe. The heel area still fit. She replaced the buttons and patched a small hole in a sweater I had outgrown - it was Peter's gift. There was no big Christmas dinner, but Grandfather had managed to get a fish for each of his sons' families. Of course, there was a church service to honor the birth of the Christ child. That was the only normal part of Christmas that year and the four that followed.

January and February, the coldest months in Chios, are rainy. The average temperature is 50 degrees, but dampness makes it seem colder. Sitting near the fireplace was the best seat in my home as well as at Grandfather's. That position allowed me warmth, and I could listen to the adults talk about the news in the village and from the hidden radios.

The Germans had differing ways of dealing with traitors. Twin sixteen-year-old boys destroyed a part of German communication lines. They were caught and taken out in the ocean in a small boat. Ropes were put around them and weights put on their feet and they were thrown overboard while family watched from the shore. The Germans were still looking for the guilty party responsible for blowing up their ammunition. They were harsher about enforcing the curfew and checked everyone's papers more carefully.

In March the rains stopped and our planting salvaged seeds in secluded places gave hope of some vegetables in the summer. When the Germans destroyed Grandfather's fields, he cleared and planted an area that was out of German view. Near that field in the brush was a nanny goat the Germans hadn't found, and she had a baby that summer. Grandfather gave Mother and me the job of keeping the goat and baby hidden. In the winter they had been in an old shed behind our house. Mother checked on them before dawn and when the baby was weaned Mother milked after dark. Finding safe pasture for them was the solution to our keeping the goats. As March neared its end, I turned five.

More was expected of me. I was "the man of the house." Mother and I took turns moving the goats from place to place, never leaving them in the same spot two days in a row. Always that place had to be secluded. The nanny was giving more milk due to her improved diet. Mother was able to make cheese – even some to share.

One spring evening Mother, Peter in his stroller, and I walked into the village. Mother had bread and cheese to give to a poor widow who had no family other than a niece not yet twenty. It was just before twilight and we had enough time to get to the lady's house, stay a short time, and because dark came early in the spring, get home before the curfew.

Two houses from where we were going, a man suddenly stepped out of the shadows and blocked our way. He had his coat collar pulled high at his neck and his black cap came over his eyebrows. The rest of his face was blackened. Mother was startled, and I think, holding her breath. Before she spoke, the man whispered, "Angie". I heard Mother releasing her breath. "Are you going in that house?" He pointed at the widow's house.

Mother nodded "Yes."

"It is getting dark. Don't stay more than fifteen minutes. Promise me?"

Mother said, "Yes." The man disappeared into the alley.

"Costa, don't be afraid. The widow will be glad to see us."

We knocked on the door and a very pretty girl answered. Mother asked if her aunt was home. The girl opened the door wide, told us to come in, and led us to the kitchen where her aunt was. The older woman welcomed us and asked us to sit down; then she spoke to her niece, "You look so pretty tonight, Marie. Surely you aren't going out. It is too close to curfew."

"Someone is coming here, Auntie."

"When do I get to meet this 'someone' who comes for you before curfew and brings you back after curfew? I fear you will be caught and the Germans will put you in prison or worse."

"Don't worry, the Germans won't hurt me. Did you eat the supper I brought you?"

When the widow said, "Yes", the girl left the room.

My mother told the widow we brought her bread and cheese, but couldn't stay because of the curfew. She said she understood and was grateful for the food. Then she said, "Marie sometimes brings me food I have never before tasted. It is different but good. When I asked her where it came from, she avoided an answer. She is a grown up now and has her own life."

We got home about five minutes before curfew.

Retribution

Through the winter months, even when it was raining, I practiced hitting a target on the stone wall with the slingshot Grandfather had given me. I was certain I could hunt and bring home food for us. As proof, I shot a bird out of a bush and proudly presented it to Mother. Startled at first, she asked, "Why are you bringing me a dead bird?"

Her voice sounded so sad and tears were ready to spill from her eyes, and I thought, "Mother, why are you crying over this?" Instead I said, "Mother, I killed it with my slingshot. I know it is too little for our supper, but I wanted you to know I am a good shooter."

"Well done, my Costa."

"Mother, is something wrong?"

"Yes, I just got sad news from Aunt Jenny. She stayed only long enough to tell me. The widow's niece, the girl you met last night, is dead. Now the widow has no one to help her."

"What happened to her?"

"She was shot. That is all I will say. Go, bury the bird." She motioned me out the door.

Only the Germans have guns, I thought, so she must have been caught out after curfew. Then I decided to show Grandfather my trophy to prove I could use his gift accurately.

I didn't knock. I just opened the door, called his name, and walked toward the kitchen where I saw him standing –leaning against a tall cabinet as though he was too weak to stand, head drooping, not looking well. Great-uncle Michael and his friend Fotus were there too. As I entered the kitchen, Uncle Michael was quietly but angrily saying, "She killed them…" He stopped talking when he saw me.

Then there were seconds of silence before Grandfather said, "Costa, what do you need?"

"I want you to know I can use my slingshot to hunt. See?" I held up the dead bird. "I shot it out of a bush. I know I can get food for us now."

"I can use your help to provide. What did your mother tell you to do with the bird?"

"She told me to bury it, but I wanted you to see that I am a good shot. I will do what she asked now."

After supper, I told Mother what Uncle Michael had said and then I asked, "You told me the widow's niece was shot and she is dead. Did she kill someone and then she died? Was Uncle Michael talking about that 'she'?"

"Yes, the same one. She did not shoot anyone. Before you ask me your next question, I am reminding you to not talk about this with anyone, not even Grandfather."

"Okay."

"The widow's niece gave the Germans information that caused them to arrest two young Greeks and kill them for blowing up the German supply truck and the storage barn."

"But she didn't kill them the Germans did, so what did Unc....?"

"Costa, her giving the Germans their description and the time when they hung around the docks was insuring, they would be killed. And I don't know who killed her, but I do know anyone who gives the Germans information about the Greek resistance puts many, many people in danger of dying."

"Mother, are we safe - and Grandfather and Grandmother and the aunts and cousins – are we safe?"

"Yes, Costa, what did I tell you? Remember, Jesus watches over us."

Good Fortune

Peter and I went with Mother to the home of one of my aunts to share the last of our garden produce with her. This particular aunt wasn't known for her generosity, but Mother said we should be the model to show others a better way of living. So mother was giving.

Peter and I played in the yard while waiting for Mother. I spotted a tree, a very climbable tree- beside Aunt's house. I called Peter to come watch me as I scooted up the tree to a thick limb and dangled my feet above Peter's head. He jumped up and down yelling, "Me too, me too." I told him he was too little, and he started to cry softly at first then got louder. I swung my left leg over to the tree trunk and as my body turned, I looked through a small window into Aunt's pantry.

Peter now hit a volume that brought Mother running from the house. I dropped to the ground as she reached Peter and demanded to know the problem. I explained while she examined Peter for blood. No blood, really no problem and a stern, "Enough, Peter!", and we were on our way home.

That night I made a plan. In the morning, I did my chores and asked Mother if I could go out until she needed me to watch Peter. I made a run to the tree beside Aunt's house but was careful to not be in view of the windows. When I got to the position that had made Peter cry, I carefully slid to the end of the branch and leaned down. The window in the pantry was hinged like a door. My fingers touched it and it opened. From there it was easy to get into the pantry. Here and there on the shelves were jars of canned goods, but yesterday I had seen seven jars of fruit jams. I reached for one, removed the lid and helped myself to the jam. I was careful to only eat the contents in the middle of the jar, put the lid on, and replace the jar in its same position. I did that another time and then climbed out the window, onto the tree limb, down the tree and went home. What a treat. I was already planning my next trip.

Several days later I dined again. All the jars looked full, but I knew which I had eaten from. About a week later, I made a third trip. I had to make this last so I decided on only one jar at a time. I placed the jar on the shelf, and had one leg out the window when the pantry door opened and there was Aunt and my mother and Peter.

Mother's modeling good works caused Aunt to give her a jar of jam. Aunt invited Mother to have a cup of herb tea and while the water was heating Mother opened the jam jar and gasped. Aunt looked at her and Mother held the jar so Aunt could see the empty middle, with the remaining jam showing the track of a small finger.

Now they were looking at me. Mother removed me from the window. When we got home, she got the belt. It hurt. I tried not to cry. I did, a little. Peter made up for it. He screamed and cried until Mother stopped swinging the belt. Later Mother and I talked. My only defense was, "I am hungry." At that, my Mother's eyes filled with tears, she hugged me, and told me to dry the dishes.

Sharp Shooter

At five, I had become an excellent marksman. I had asked God to make my shots straight and true. My ammunition was imperfect ball bearings the Germans were going to melt down and reuse. The collection barrels for them were near the docks. When full, the barrels were put on German ships and sent back to German factories. Grandfather would find excuses to walk by that area in case some bearings had fallen to the ground. If so, he would accidently trip and pick up the treasure. Over a period of two weeks using various methods, he had collected about a dozen. Together he and I painted the bearings red so I wouldn't lose them.

Grandfather showed me how to make a fish trap using my mother's bread kneading trough weighted down with rocks in shallow water. We put a net with a small hole in it tightly around the trough. The fish would swim in and then were not able to get out. There was only one flaw in this set up − Mother didn't want her wooden trough saturated with fishy water. I collected lily pads from the pond and scraped the frog eggs from them for Mother to cook. I learned how to catch fish by lying submerged, except for my face, until one swam across my chest. Then I would grab it and put it in a burlap bag.

Mother had planted about an acre of wheat, and after it was harvested, Grandfather and I took the gleanings and spread them on a marble slab we had dragged into the field. When the birds gathered to eat the wheat, we dropped a fish net on them.

In the clear shallow waters of the Aegean Sea, it was easy to see the bottom. I made a harpoon with a fork tied to a stick so I could spear eels for Mother and Grandfather. I seemed to always be hungry, but I would not eat eels. I was sure they would jump around in my stomach the way they did in the frying pan.

The first time I brought down seagulls, I proudly presented them to my mother who cooked them for supper. They were stringy, tough and greasy. "No more of these!" declared my mother. Sea Gulls were put into the same category as rats.

My mother worked for the Flamous family who had been financially well-off before the war. In addition to wages, they gave Mother a plate of food to bring home to Peter and me. Money for food wasn't the need. The hard fact was that there was no food to be had. That situation only got worse. I remember the pain of always being hungry.

Sharp Shooter

Resistance Enlistment

I not only knew my grandfather's fields and the surrounding neighbors' fields; I also knew our shore line. Because my slingshot, harpoon and I were always on the lookout for food, I had gone beyond the village shore line to the base of the mountains. There are caves in our mountains and places where the Aegean flows into the caves. I had come to one of those watery entrances and heard voices inside. There was no sign of any boat or German troops anywhere so I went inside and followed the sound. I was seen before I saw them, my eyes had not adjusted to the dim light. Then a voice said, "It is ok. This is Costa."

It was Uncle Michael's voice, Grandfather's brother, and I recognized his friend, Fotus. It was then that I noticed the other men had pulled their caps low on their faces and had pulled their neck scarves higher on their faces.

After the Germans took over the Island of Chios, it was no time until the Resistance began chipping away at their plans. I had a glimpse of "The Resistance" one night in Vrontados. Now I was standing in the midst of them. My eyes were now adjusted to the low light, but I was startled by the voice of a woman. My head jerked so quickly in her direction that Uncle Michael, along with several others, laughed out loud.

Then I heard a voice, "Young man, may I introduce my wife." I nodded. That nod made me a six-year-old gun runner. Those two had a two- person submarine. I never knew their names. They spoke Greek, but with a strange accent. Their submarine could move undetected in the waters and surface inside the cave to unload the guns and ammunition. Then men and boys were needed to carry the supplies up inside the mountain to the fighters. I carried a rifle and a box of ammunition in my sack with the fish I had caught. I don't know how the path got inside the mountain. Some places looked recently chiseled, other places the rock was worn down by usages. Some places were narrow and steep. When we got to the top, I was not allowed outside of the mountain. Uncle Michael took what I had carried, and told me to not move from where I was. Some of the men stayed with the Resistance group.

Back at the sea, Fotus warned me not to tell anyone what I had seen or done.

Several weeks later, I walked in on a conversation between Grandfather and his brother Michael. I had not heard what they had said, but Fotus had followed me in and he said, "Michael, ready? They may be waiting." They turned to leave and I followed.

"Costa," said Grandfather as his hand pulled back on my shirt, "No more. Understand?"

The sternness of his voice made me say, "I understand."

Hitch Hiking

From time to time, without Mother or Grandfather's permission, I would go to Chios Town- Chora. An older friend and I knew that a neighbor, an old man who was also hard of hearing, went to Chora in his horse drawn wagon most every Monday. We had been practicing chasing his wagon, which was not going faster than a slow trot, ducking under it and riding the four miles by hanging from the cross beams with our fingers and toes. We would just let go when we neared the town and the old man never knew we were there. So it was on Monday, February 7, 1944.

The purpose for our mission was food. Finding food has been the priority of every day since the end of 1941 and that situation had become worse as time moved on. We had heard the adults talk about a Greek freighter bringing grain that might be docking in Chora on Monday. We intended to take home some of that grain using the tools my friend had brought: a knife and his book sack. The freighter was docked beside a Red Cross ship carrying the wounded.

Our timing was perfect. The men had just begun carrying the sacks to a truck parked further up the dock in front of some buildings. There were people everywhere: counting, carrying, giving orders, and of course the Germans checking people's paperwork. The more focused they were on their own business, the better for us. My friend would wander in behind the man with the grain sack over his shoulder and slit the sack, drop out of the way, return to our starting point, and I would step in with the open book sack to catch the grain, then move aside. It took maybe twenty seconds. We would wait until another two men passed then do it all over again after checking to see if anyone was paying attention to us. Each time it seemed we were getting a little closer to the truck before we stepped aside.

On the fourth go at it, the sound of planes and falling bombs were simultaneous and the Red Cross ship exploded! I dived into a nearby basement doorway. My friend dropped to the ground. He suffered the loss of his arm, I was bruised and cut, but nothing serious. I remember seeing body parts on the dock and people rushing to help, but I don't remember how my friend got help or how I got home. I do remember the sound of the German planes. They thought the Red Cross ship was carrying guns and ammunition to the Greek Resistance, but it was carrying wounded Greek. I remember it was Monday, February 7, 1944.

The Box

The rapid pounding on the front door brought me from the kitchen but not before my mother flung the door open to face Aunt Jenny. She was pale and her voice shook as she clutched my mother's shoulders and said, "The Germans are going house to house looking for young boys. They have taken fifteen-year-old Paulus and Thon who just turned ten. Angie, hide Costa!" She was gone before I could process what she was talking about. I turned to see Mother emptying an old wooden box. That's what I called it, but Mother said it was a steamer trunk that had belonged to her aunt.

"Costa, get in here, now!" she pointed, "There is a gap where the side meets the front. Put your head there – against that side."

My mother's tone scared me and I did what she said. She spread a blanket over my curled body and tucked other items from the box around me. "Don't move," she ordered, "Don't make a sound – not until I open the lid. Costa, do you understand me?"

I didn't, but I whispered, "Yes." Aunt Jenny had said, "Germans." I had seen what they would do if they were not immediately obeyed.

Mother rushed around placing other things that had been in the trunk. She stacked books on the lid. The slit in the corner of my box allowed me to see enough to know Mother wanted nothing to look unusual.

The heavy knocking came as the order to open the door was barked in German- accented Greek. Mother was greeted with, "Good day, Madame. Where is your son?"

Her voice was surprisingly calm. "Costa? He is out in the fields somewhere with his friends. When the weather is like this they are gone for hours."

"Perhaps he has returned without your knowing. Of course, you won't mind if we look," the man in charge sneered and gave orders to the other two. I heard their clopping upstairs and through the downstairs.

Black leather darkened my line of vision. From the sound, I knew he had picked up a book. Silence. I clamped my hand over my mouth and held my breath. A sudden crash on the top of the box broke the silence, and the book thumped to the floor. I bit my tongue bloody holding back a scream. The German's black leather boot kicked the book against the side of the box, and he laughed as he did so.

The one in charge spoke to his men in German; then in Greek to my mother and said, "We will be back." The front door slammed and I waited for Mother to open the lid, but she didn't. I heard her washing dishes, dusting, and sweeping the floors. Why was she leaving me in this box? The light coming through the crack told me it was late afternoon. I had been in the box for hours and hours – since before lunch. My legs were numb. I needed water instead of the taste of blood. My head ached and I was still shaking.

Again, there was a knock at the door. The door opened and a woman's cheerful voice called, "Evangeline, Angie, I brought you something." Mother came. The woman continued, "I just took this from the oven and knew you would like it hot."

Mother sighed the sound of relief and said, "Bless you." The woman left. The lock clicked on the door, and the lid of my box was opened.

That was the first but not the last concealment in the box. Mother and I learned how to make my stay in the box easier than that first time, but the fear – the fear never lessened.

The Box

Out and About

By the time summer came in full, I wanted to be outside. When I wasn't with Grandfather or helping Mother, I was out. Sometimes I had a friend to play with. One of those times I thought the Germans were going to come after us and I would never see my home again.

I knew Grandfather's land well and I knew the fields around them. That day my friend and I wandered farther than usual on the mountainside, and discovered a German tank that had been disabled by the Greek Resistance fighters. We climbed inside, and I took a seat nearer the front and my friend seated himself behind me but on a higher level. I tried the levers until I found one that moved; it moved the long gun in the front. I could swing the gun back and forth. In a serious and deep tone I said, "The enemy is coming, are you ready corporal?"

My friend responded with, "Yes Sir." At the same time he said that, I swung the gun again and pulled the trigger. The blast from the gun lifted me out of my seat. My friend jumped up, hit his head, and screamed, "Let's go!"

I was holding on to the firing mechanism, unable to let go. Both of us were screaming as the firing continued. Finally the gun was empty. We scrambled to get out and ran and ran to get home. Surely the German heard the shooting. Surely, they would be looking for somebody. They didn't, they weren't. I don't recall any backlash from the incident. We agreed to not tell anyone.

I wasn't ever again going to get into a German tank, but there was a forbidden ride I was delighted to take. When Grandfather had to go to Chora, he allowed me to go along, usually. The ancient windmills were the reason I wanted to go. They were built on an arm of the land that stretched a short distance into the Aegean; four of them, made of stone, each a slightly different size or shape. However, when the windmill turned, the paddles came within a few feet of the ground – just a stretching jump for me to grab a hold and be hoisted into the air. Part of the reason for this stunt was to give me bragging rights. When one of my friends was in Chora, his story was how long he managed to hang on. We had agreed on a rhythmic count and the highest number made the hero.

I chose the shortest one so, except for the very top of the cycle, even if I had to let go at any point, the drop to the ground wasn't far. I had been trying to hang on, but was having to let go before the top and I was on the ground on my back twice. My count was only five so far. A short distance from me were two German soldiers laughing and pointing at me.

I got up and waited until just the right paddle to latch onto came to me. I reached and held, got to five, at six my hands slipped and I landed on my back, but had the wind knocked out of me. I opened my eyes to see the soldiers standing above me. I didn't even have time to be scared because Grandfather was lifting me to my feet and said, " I need to get him home!" Grandfather threw me over his shoulder, and with the full width of his long stride got me out of there. It wasn't until the war ended that I got to try that again.

Out and About

Miracle Worker

The Greek patriots, the resistance fighters, worked to undermine and destroy the Germans. Every day there was sniper activity. Starvation was as deadly as a bullet to the heart. Peter's speech and muscular development were delayed because of malnutrition. I knew, because of my mother and our family and friends, that our faith had deepened. There was nothing or no one to trust or believe in except Jesus Christ, who had suffered much more than we were. God worked miracles through those most difficult times, and I was the receiver of one of them.

In March of 1945, I turned eight and it was spring and outdoor game time. I was a strong runner and played a good game of soccer in any open field. We had neither uniforms nor soccer shoes. Whoever wanted to play made up the teams. During one of those games, I got a hard kick to my left shin by a teammate who had found a worn pair of spiked shoes.

My mother took me to the hospital in Chora. Although the staff was mostly Greek, the hospital was run by Germans. It was a German doctor who looked at my leg. He looked at my mother and said, "I have no time to deal with this. Go!"

Mother took me to a midwife in Vrontados who put bamboo sticks on either side of my leg and wound cloth around it. Days later I woke to a horrible smell and screamed for Mother. She came running and unwrapped the bandages. The flesh of my leg was black and rotting. The bone was showing.

Mother took Peter and ran for Grandfather. Grandmother kept Peter and Grandfather brought his wagon and lifted me in. Again, we went to the hospital. It was a different but German doctor who looked at my leg. He answered my mother's look with, "I can cut off his leg at the knee. I cannot save his leg, but I can save his life."

With tears overflowing and determination in her voice, she responded, "No! You can't. He is a runner." She and Grandfather took me home.

Even then I believed God had control over our disasters. Sometime after that -I don't know how long- my Godfather came to visit. He was a well-known neurosurgeon from Vrontados who traveled Europe with a neutral visa. Of course, he looked at my leg. He was the one who had taught the midwife how to wrap wounds, and so was surprised at what he saw. He told Mother to put me on the kitchen table because my leg had to be cut off.

Again, she said, "No! You do your job and God will do His."

My aunt arrived. She and Mother tied me to the kitchen table and gave me whiskey to drink - no anesthetic. Mother stood by the doctor to assist him and my aunt put one hand on my forehead and in the other, she had a folded washcloth. I was screaming. Holding the cloth to my mouth, she said, "Bite!"

The doctor began to cut. Maybe it was at that point I passed out. Later, when she knew I could handle it, Mother told me, "Costa, the doctor cut away the dead flesh, took skin from your thigh and used that along with good skin around the wound pulled over the opening then burned them together with a hot iron. We boiled strips of a sheet to use as bandages." There was no ointment, no antibiotic.

Grandfather told Mother to put me in the sun every day.

Miracle Worker Part 2

I spent the next weeks of my life in an open field propped up on a cot. The sun warmed my bandages. I was not able to even get up from the cot by myself. I had bread and water to last until Mother came for me.

The German pilots continued their intimidation tactic of flying low over whomever and machine-gunning around the area. I was discovered by a German Stuka pilot. He opened fire in a wide circle around me. Each day after that, the Germans played the same torture game – fly in, drop low, and fire all around me. By the third day, I recognized the distant noise of the Stuka engine. The ring of fire seemed to get closer with each show.

Then came the day I heard the plane engine and I knew I was going to die. I had been afraid at first. Now my Mother's words gave me courage, "Do not be afraid, my son. Jesus and your saint will protect you." I knew God loved me. I believed that. The plane was almost over me. Out of nowhere, a hummingbird landed on my shoulder. The plane dropped down to shoot and the bird flew away. The plane circled the cot, climbed, and also flew away. He did not return. I know the hummingbird was God's sign. I was saved from German ammunition. I knew my leg was healed. My injury occurred in late March. Soon after the hummingbird appeared, I was out of the field and the month was May. On May 7, 1945, Germany surrendered to the Allies. WW2 was over!

And He will Protect You

By December I didn't need the crutch so much, but I still had pain. Some of my friends came to wish me a Merry Christmas and they sang *The Little Drummer Boy*. For whatever reason, that is a vivid memory.

The Germans were taking their time leaving Chios. WW2 was over, but a civil war broke out between the Greeks who wanted a Republic and the Greek Communists. So, killing still happened, and food was still scarce. America would be safe.

My mother began the necessary paperwork to get us there. She had an aunt in New York who would sponsor us. Mother was an American citizen born in Philadelphia, Pennsylvania. Her parents died when she was nine and an aunt had brought her to Greece, to Chios.

Once the official documents were completed, passage to Athens was arranged. We were going to stay with a relative for three days then board a refitted American Landing Support Troop (LST) ship. Mother told us things about America, but it was like a puzzle picture with too many missing pieces. Peter and I had never been farther from Vrontados than Chora. The one thing I knew for certain was that God would be there with us.

Mother made us understand that the relatives in Athens were really sacrificing to have us stay with them for three days, and warned us that our normal rowdiness would get us in deep trouble. The eight-hour trip to Athens ended in disappointing news. The Marine Shark had to undergo repairs estimated to take two weeks. Three extra people for two weeks was too much to expect. I had to go back to Grandfather for the next two weeks. Mother found an acquaintance, named John, who was sailing his schooner back to his home on Chios. I would also return to Athens with him.

Mother hugged me, then gently pushed me in front of her. Still having her hands cupping my shoulders, she looked me in the eyes and said, "Costa this is not an easy thing I am asking of you, but I feel I have no choice. I will pray and ask Jesus to protect you and send Saint Isidoros to watch over you. Do not be afraid."

I reached out to hug her again and firmly stated, "I am not afraid."

It was a full moon when the ship docked in Chora. John offered, "Costa, it is late and has been a long trip. You may stay the night with me and go your way in the morning."

"Thank you, but no. It is only a 45- minute walk to Grandfather's then I will be where I need to be."

"Remember, you must be here at 9:00 in the morning in exactly 13 days." I assured him I would. Then I began walking.

In Vrontados I stopped at my church to pray that all would be well for me to stay with Grandfather, and that I would get back to my mother safely. I had only walked a short distance when I heard the sound of horse's hooves on cobblestones behind me, but I was walking on a dirt road. I turned, but there was nothing there and no sound. When I walked, I heard the horse's hooves. When I stopped, the sound stopped. There was nothing behind me. This continued until I came to an aunt's house before reaching Grandfather's. I pounded on the door. My aunt opened the door and jerked me in. With wide eyes and hurried breathing, she spurted out, "What are you doing here, and do you know who is behind you!?"

In one big breath, I blurted, "Aunt, the ship needed repairs and there is a horse behind me, but I cannot see it."

"Isidoros was behind you on a white horse and in his full armor!!"

In the morning, I went to Grandfather's. Approaching the front door, I heard men's loud voices. I knew one was Grandfather's, but I didn't know the other until he yelled, "But he is MY son. She can't take him!" I ran back to Aunt Jenny's house and told her what I had heard. I stayed with her until she knew my father was gone.

Going, Going, Gone

Grandfather drove me to Chora in his wagon. He greeted John and thanked him for bringing me to Chios and for taking me back to Athens. All of a sudden Grandfather hugged me to himself, and I hugged his middle. We both let go at the same time, and he said, "Costa, take care of your mother and Peter. Remember us." I nodded and hugged him again.

John said, "Time to go."

I looked up at Grandfather and he quietly said, "Yes."

In Athens, all three of us had to get shots and take medicine to kill intestinal worms, and give us immunity against diseases. Finally, we boarded the ship.

About that part of my life, I left behind - it was not a normal, "what a childhood should be" life. I had no shoes. My feet were wrapped with burlap bags and newspaper. I was hungry all the time. My Grandfather was the best father I did not have. My mother taught me about God and said, "Do not be afraid, Jesus Christ and your Saint are with you." And they were and are. My mother was a pillar of light in that life. She trusted God. That's all we had.

Crossing the Atlantic was treacherous because of mines. We had several drills in case we hit one. We practiced getting into life jackets and going to the deck side in a calm orderly way then reviewed how we would get into the lifeboats. The crew took turns being assigned to the wooden row boat that stayed in front of the ship to look for the explosives. There were other Greek children on board and Peter and I played with them. There were not a few times that we got in trouble with the adults. The whole trip was so very different from what life had been.

After two weeks at sea, we docked at Ellis Island. Again, we were examined by doctors. Peter and I were very thin, but healthy. The first thing that caught my attention was the statue of a woman holding a basket of fruits and vegetables. The interpreter explained that the basket of food represented abundance, plenty of everything good. We spent almost a week getting examined, being questioned, and waiting for the process to be completed. At last Mother had our approved papers. We crossed by ferry to New York City where Mother's aunt met us.

Coming to America would be a new life with good things.

Found in a box belonging to Costa's mother were three certificates of vaccination against smallpox signed by a physician in Athens, Greece on August 3, 1946. Also found were passenger tickets from American Export lines-Inc. dated July 31, 1946, for $334 for three Moushouri to sail on the SS "Marine Carp" scheduled to leave on August 10, 1946. However, the Boarding Control assigning Berth is for the SS "Marine Shark."

Both of these LSTs were refitted after WW2 to carry passengers. Landing ship, Tank, or Tank Landing Ship is the navel designation for ships first developed during WW2 (1939-1945) to support amphibious operations by carrying tanks, vehicles, cargo, and landing troops directly on the shore with no docks or piers. This enabled assaults on almost any beach.

Above is the passport picture from Evangeline Moushouri, and her two sons Costa and Peter.

Epilogue

Costa entered the New York Public Schools system when he was almost nine and a half years old and placed in second grade. By the end of the year, he was placed in his age-grade level. He was teased because he was different. He didn't speak English, was from Greece and he spoke Greek. From that, came the nickname "Gus" and it stuck.

The stories "Miracle Worker" and "Miracle Worker Part 2" were the prologue for saving Gus's life. When I met him, he was in his eleventh year of being a heart transplant recipient. The average lifespan for heart transplant receivers was 9.16 years at that time. The doctors knew his damaged left leg would have weak veins so they planned to take veins from the healthy right leg during surgery. However, they were wrong. It was the left leg that had the best veins. Gus gave God the credit for saving his leg in childhood so his life could be saved in adulthood.

Gus told me many things about his life after coming to America. Not all of them brought honor to God, but God – Jesus and his saint were never far from his thoughts. Perhaps those are stories for another time.

.

ADDITIONAL

INFORMATION

Chios

Google Chios, Greece and any number of travel agencies will come up such as All Over Greece at **https://www.allovergreece.com** . There will be many beautiful pictures of the island and the Aegean Sea. Or you might even order a guidebook such as <u>Chios, The Fragrant Island</u> from **http://www.toubis.gr** from which comes this quote and other information that follows.

"The island of mastic, jasmine, and intoxicating fragrances, the island of orchards and orange groves, the noble island with its stone mansions and their pebbled courtyards, with its unique medieval villages and their towers. There is no other place like Chios in the Aegean." *(Mastic is a resin from the mastic tree. It has many uses including in medicine.)*

The Greek islands number 6,000. Of the largest five islands, Chios is the fifth in size. The economy of the island is dependent upon the production of mastic and other agricultural goods. Fishing and animal husbandry add to that. It has a Mediterranean climate with summer temperatures not exceeding 82.4 degrees Fahrenheit, and winters no colder than 50 degrees Fahrenheit in mid-January. Rainfall is rare, especially in the summer, but there is underground water that surfaces in clear springs or is drawn from wells. In fact, in the mountains on the island, there are caves with waters flowing like rivers that are accessible from the sea. *(Costa's story of a small two-person submarine emerging to the surface inside a cave is every bit possible.)*

Now about Costa's village, Vrontados is located less than 4 miles north of Chios Town and is known for its notable maritime traditions. In Costa's time, many of the men were fishermen and seafarers.

Greek Merchant Marine

By definition, *britannica.*com/topic/merchant-marine say, " The merchant marine are the commercial ships of a nation, whether privately or publicly owned. The term merchant marine also denotes the personnel that operate such ships, as distinct from the personnel of naval vessels, Merchant ships are used to transport people, raw materials, and manufactured goods. Merchant fleets can be important economic assets for nations that have limited natural resources or a relatively small industrial base. By carrying the commerce of other nations on the seas, a merchant fleet contributes to its home nation's foreign-exchange earnings, promotes trade, and provides employment."

In an October 23, 2023 article written by Alexander Billinis, found at greekreporter.com>Greece>Greek Mariner Fought the Axis Power Long Before OXI Day, the reporter documents the Greeks had the ninth largest merchant marine in the world. Greece remained neutral when Hitler declared war in September 1939, and continued to say, "No." (OXI) to the Axis powers while transporting goods to England and other Allied countries. The Greek Merchant Marine was a target for German U-boats and mines in the seas. Ships were sunk and men died.

The merchant marines carried supplies to all areas of the fighting. They were an integral part of large-scale transportation of military units from one front to another: North Africa, Sicily, Anzio, southern France, and Normandy. They evacuated trapped units, ran blockades, and did their job of bringing supplies.

Costa's father and his brothers were a part of this. Consult this article for more detailed information.

Not Fishing

The village men were told to bring their guns to the police station. It was a new ordinance, but when they needed their guns, they could take them, then again return them to the police station. That was a lie. When they heard the Germans were coming into the harbor, they ran to get their guns, but not even one gun was there.

In the book, <u>Gun Control in the Third Reich: Disarming the Jews and "Enemies of the State,"</u> author Stephen P. Halbrook writes about the systematic removal of guns from the Germans. In 1933 Adolf Hitler was in control of Germany. He suspended constitutional rights, used gun registration records to disarm the people, and initiated seizures of their guns. In 1938 Hitler signed a New Gun Control Act. It restricted Jews from working in the firearms industry and banned the sale of .22 caliber hollow-point ammunition. France fell to Nazi occupation in 1940 and the French no longer had freedom of speech or the right to own guns. The Germans killed any Frenchman who did comply.

In trying to find substantial proof for the taking of Greek guns before the Germans invaded, I have only Costa's words. However, the Fascist elements in the Greek government may have been behind that gun collection. Nevertheless, disarmament was the first order for all German-occupied countries. A disarmed population is easier to suppress.

Halbrook, Stephen P., Gun Control in the Third Reich: Disarming the Jews and "Enemies of the State," Independent Institute. January 2014.

The Patron Saint of Chios, Saint Isidoros

In 250 A.D., in the reign of Decius, the Roman fleet under the command of Admiral Noumerianos arrived in Chios. A young Greek man, Isideros, from Alexandria, saw service in the fleet. Isideros was a quartermaster sergeant and a devout Christian. Isideros and his Christian friend, Amenios, stayed in a house in the region of Kampos. When he prayed to God in the night, lightning and flames could be seen over the roof of his house. Many of his neighbors were impressed and were convinced by Isideros and Amenios that all that light was divine and they were baptized Christians. The news was spread quickly. Admiral Noumerianos also heard about it and so he called for Isideros. He accused him of not sacrificing to the gods. Isideros' reply was regarded to have been offensive and Noumerianos asked that Isideros be beheaded. After whipping and dragging him chained on a horse, the Romans cut off his head on May 14th 250 A.D. Isideros' head was found by a Christian Woman from Ephesus, Miropi, and she buried it with his body. She was discovered and martyred for her action. In the fifth century A.D., the Chians built a temple just above his grave.

ORTHODOX CHRISTIANITY THEN AND NOW
https://www.johnsanidopoulos.com

Third Century Saint

This was difficult to believe- a 3rd-century soldier protecting a 20th-century child! However, when skeptically sharing Costa's telling of this memory with a friend of mine, she said, "What if he had said an angel was following him? Would you have as much trouble believing that?"

A change of perspective was needed.

In the early 1990s, Gus (the adult Costa) and his wife went to Vrontados, Chios, Greece. They met with Costa's cousins and many other family members. As the family shared stories and histories, they told about the time Costa returned to the aunt's house. She had indeed opened the door to see Saint Isideros behind Costa.

I leave the reader with that verification to decide for yourself.

Strange Visit

It seemed necessary to make use of creative license to make a chronological story for the reader. *Broken to Pieces, Something Missing, It Worked* and the inclusion of two unkempt young men's interaction with Grandfather in *Fish Thieves* were a necessary made-up bridge to *Strange Visit.* In Costa's telling of this happening, he related that Marie, age eighteen, was engaged to a resistance fighter. But because of being fearful of starvation, she entertained the attention of a German officer who provided food for her and her aunt. Whether the officer was more clever than Maria, or Maria unknowingly talked too much and gave names of men in the resistance. It matters little. Within fifteen minutes of Costa and his mother's leaving the widow, the black-faced, black-garbed Greek Resistance fighters entered the widow's house, took Marie to the roof, and shot her.

Not knowing any of the facts of the sabotage attack made by the resistance that ended in the death of resistance fighters and a young woman, I created a scenario that included a motorcycle. Historically, the Germans confiscated or destroyed all motorized vehicles during their occupation so a hidden one carried the storyline...

About that motorcycle; it was a BMW. Translated into English it stands for Bavarian Motor Works. Bavaria is a southern state in Germany where the BMW company began. Creative license requires research and the question was, "Were motorcycles available in the mid 1920's?"

In 1923 the BMW R32 had a top speed of 59 mph and had a recirculating oil system while other makes used a total loss system. Ernst Henne, part of the BMW team, supercharged that model into the R37 which had a top speed of 115 mph. So that was the sabotage vehicle. How did it get to Chios? No problem if you have more than enough money – before the stock market crash of 1929.

The Box

I have no verification of the Germans conscripting children of the occupied countries for the Hitler Youth. I believe Costa's recollection and I do believe Nazi brutality was reason enough for mothers to hide their children when the Nazis came looking for anything.

Much information about Hitler Youth can be found at The History Place. Recruits were boys and girls ages ten to eighteen. Hitler conscripted children for his program in other countries if there was a large German population in that country. Both boys and girls had extensive physical training to exhibit their superiority – boys for military and girls for motherhood (they would be the first to instill the German worldview). The real goal was indoctrination: Germans are the superior race. Inferior peoples need to be terminated.

Near the end of WW2, youths fourteen to eighteen were armed for battle and as the Allies advanced even younger children became soldiers. The desperate state of the German army is evident in this," American troops reported capturing armed 8-year-olds at Aachen in Western Germany and knocking out artillery units operated entirely by boys aged twelve and under. Girls were also used now, operating the 8mm anti-aircraft guns alongside the boys." (from The History Place site)

This information and much more detail can be found in encyclopedias, visiting the Holocaust Museum in Washington D.C., or googling historyplace.com/worldwar2/hitler youth/hj-boy-soldiers.html

The Greek Famine

German occupation of Greece officially began on April 27, 1941, when the Germans replaced the Greek flag on the Acropolis in Athens, with the Nazi flag. Soon after that, the Germans occupied the Greek islands. Statistics may vary, but between two hundred thousand and three hundred thousand people died during the German occupation. The death rate reached its highest point during the winter of 1941-1942.

Brutality, extreme retaliation, and starvation were used by the Germans to keep the people subjugated. In cities, they plundered the grocery stores. In the rural areas, they stripped the fields or destroyed them. They took animals, or they destroyed them. The Allies had blockaded Greece and the black- market had become a powerful source selling to the highest bidder. The result was starvation for the Greek people.

Greek-Australian Violetta Hionidou, professor of Modern European history at the University of Newcastle in the UK, has authored Famine and Death in Occupied Greece, 1941-1942 She stated, "Most of the photographs and accounts are from Athens – but Athens did not suffer the most, Mykonos, Syros, and **CHOIS** (emphasis mine) certainly suffered more." An excerpt and review of her book can be found at
https://muse.jhu.edu/article/253490/pdf .

Hiondou, Violetta, Famine and Death in Occupied Greece, 1941-1944, Cambridge University Press, July 2006.

Resistance Enlistment

In search of information to support Costa's experience with the resistance, I found the Long-Range Desert Group. It was a reconnaissance and raiding unit of the British Army during WW2 formed to carry out deep penetration, and intelligence missions from behind enemy lines. In 1943 the Axis forces surrendered in Tunisia and the Group was relocated from desert areas to the eastern Mediterranean carrying out missions in the Greek Islands, Italy, and the Balkans.

The people who comprised this group were regularly parachuted into enemy-held islands or came by sea in stormy darkness and may have operated for long periods of time as spies, saboteurs, and liaison officers with the local resistance groups. Some had their own boats based on German-held islands in the Aegean.

The LRG assisted another British Army unit called the Special Air Service Forces that specialized in counter-terrorism and hostage rescue in addition to all the LRG did. Much of the information about the SAS is highly classified by the British government and the Ministry of Defense.

In September 1942 the SAS was renamed 1st SAS Regiment which consisted of four British Squadrons and one Free French, one Greek Squadron, and the Special Boat Section. This part of the SAS operated in the Aegean.

This information is from Wikipedia, but original sources are listed at the end of the articles.

Southern Chios has hidden harbors, creeks, and inlets that made it less dangerous to avoid the German patrol boats. I couldn't find any information about a husband-wife two-man submarine. That does not mean Costa's recounting didn't happen.

Hitch Hiking

The account titled "Hitch Hiking" caused Costa and his friend to be in harm's way. Costa said a German plane attacked the ship. Research indicates it was a British plane. The target was the Swedish Red Cross ship making a humanitarian food delivery. Sweden was considered a neutral country and the *Wiril* was a hospital ship so neither the Allied forces nor the Axis powers should have attacked, but...

Shipwrecks in February 1944 include the Swedish ship *Wiril* being bombed in the harbor in Chois Town (capital of Chios). This entry is referenced to: **Rohwer, Jürgen**; Gerhard Hümmelchen. **"Seekrieg 1944, February"**. *Württembergische Landesbibliothek Stuttgart* (in German). Retrieved 31 July 2015.

Additionally, the *Birmingham Post* contained an article recounting an apology to the Swedish Government from the British Government for the plane attack on the Swedish Red Cross ship *Wiril* docked in Chios harbor on Monday, February 7, 1944.

Birmingham Daily Post
Published: Friday 11, February 1944
County: Warwickshire UK
britishnewspaperarchive.co.uk

Stuka (from Sturzkampffugzeug "dive bomber")

In Costa's story twice he told of potentially being the target of a Stuka. At first, this German plane was not equipped with the noise maker as in WW2. Sometime after the Spanish Civil War, the plane was fitted "with a wind-driven siren that uttered a banshee scream at maximum speed. The Nazis called it Jericho's Trumpet and used it to terrify people below."

The quote was taken from the University of Houston
https://engines.egr.uh.edu>episode

About the Creators

Author: Dorothy Smith is a retired elementary teacher with a desire for children to know important parts of our history. She has enjoyed using history fiction to bring facts to life for her students. Costa's World is another vehicle for entertainingly delivering facts.

Dorothy and her husband live in rural Bedford County, PA.

 If you wish to comment on this book, contact her at

dottie12@frontiernet.net

Illustrator: Joanna King is an illustrator living in the Shenandoah Valley, Virginia. She's studying digital design and illustration with Liberty University. She loves expanding her skills with new classes, new mediums and new techniques. Much of her current skills were honed in by her art teacher Nancy Marie Sessions. Joanna is inspired by the playful style of many children's books and wants to show the beautiful world we live in. Her email is joanna.king.illustrations@gmail.com for any further communications.

Cover Artist: Deanna Bussard is an illustrator based in South Central Pennsylvania, where she draws inspiration from the serene landscapes and vibrant community around her. A devoted wife and stay-at-home mother to a beautiful two-year-old daughter, Deanna skillfully balances motherhood with her passion for art. When she's not caring for her little one, she dedicates her free time to working on her creative projects, constantly exploring new techniques and styles. With a keen eye for detail and a natural talent for storytelling through visuals, Deanna's work reflects her deep love for both her family and her craft. Email her at

deannasumner13@yahoo.com

Made in United States
Cleveland, OH
12 April 2025

16040822R00043